ALTERNATIVES TO THE APPLY BUTTON

The New and Improved Way to Search For Jobs

By

Kim Brushaber

About The Author

Kim Brushaber first started working in a hiring capacity as a volunteer campus recruiter for her first job out of college. It was her responsibility to meet with potential college candidates and gather their resumes to include in a large resume book. She helped to determine which candidates should advance through the process.

She then worked for seven and a half years for a company that built Applicant Tracking Software. Applicant Tracking Software was first used to help automate the hiring process by tracking a candidate from the time they submitted their resume electronically until they signed an offer.

In 2008, Kim went to work for a recruiting firm. She helped to identify quality candidates for companies during a huge economic downturn.

In 2009, Kim started her own company, Bridge ATX where she worked with job seekers to help them find jobs during the economic downturn. She held several "Get Hired" seminars where she gathered career coaches from across Austin to come together to work with candidates to help them with all of their job search questions. She realized that the regular resources for the job search process were not helping job seekers when the market was flooded. She started "Connection Conversations" to help assist candidates with topics that were not normally covered in the variety of job seeker groups across Austin.

In 2010, Kim partnered with Austin Career Coaching to help to better equip candidates with networking skills. During this time she learned a lot from veteran career coaches while also using her knowledge to try the job search process from a different angle. She launched an executive networking job clublet that was specifically for the problems encountered by executive job seekers. She split her time between career coaching and helping companies to improve their hiring processes.

In 2011, Kim went back to work for a recruiting firm. She continues to work with job seekers in both a career coaching capacity and a headhunting capacity. Her favorite part of her week is the hour that she gets to spend with the executive job seeker group.

Alternatives to the Apply Button

Acknowledgements

Although it is impossible to acknowledge every single person I have encountered as a job seeker or a hiring manager, I would like to take a moment to thank a few specific people without whom this journey would not have been possible.

Thanks to Austin Career Coaches – Donna Fox, Stan Tyler and Pauline Hoehn for your insight into how a job search can be handled differently.

Special thanks to my copy editors – Greg Effrein, Larry Wallace, Jan Hames, Bill Herring, Paula Echols and Melanie Wise.

Another special thanks to Mark Thames, without whom I would not have been finally sparked to post this workbook online for all to use.

To all the Job Seekers out there who I have helped through Career Transitions, I hope that you are now in a job that leaves you feeling very fulfilled. If not, I hope that you continue your search until you find it.

I also need to acknowledge my family, without whom I would never have had the ambition to do this.

Alternatives to the Apply Button

Alternatives to the Apply Button

TABLE OF CONTENTS

Applying Online: The Reality

In the year 2000, I was at the very cutting edge of what has become the job seeker's bane of existence: I worked for a company that built Applicant Tracking Software. For the job seeker, this software looks like the dreaded "Apply button."The Apply button is not what it used to be; it has become a black hole that few job seekers ever make it out of. The reality is that approximately six percent of job seekers will actually be offered a position by using the online application process that starts when you click "Apply.".

In 1996, companies started taking advantage of websites for the first time. Within a few years, everyone had one. The same trend applied to companies posting their jobs online. In 2000, very few companies had online job applications. Here are some of the reasons why people chose to create this technology:

- Companies could **screen out candidates who were not technologically savvy**. Previously applications were taken via an ad in the newspaper's classifieds. Having an online tool allowed only those who were familiar with the internet to apply for the position(s).
- **Companies needed a way to handle electronic resumes**. Most companies did not post jobs on their websites. Those that did had links that allowed a job seeker to email resumes to an email account for consideration. Many companies were still taking faxed resumes. Human Resource email boxes were overflowing with resumes and it was difficult to have any visibility into the virtual pile. The online (email) system allowed companies to have an automated way to accept resumes and scan them and search for keyword matches.
- **Companies wanted a way to be able to pick up "passive job seekers."** It was a job seekers market; those who currently had a job might be willing to consider going somewhere else for the right opportunity. The online application allowed companies to build *huge* searchable databases that would take a posted job and immediately match it to the right candidates in their collected candidate pool for the company's consideration. The system saved great candidates and that could be matched against new job postings.

Things are not the same as they used to be. The technology that was available ten years ago is not an effective tool today.

Here's the current online job posting process:

1) **A hiring manager has an open position for a job.** Most recruiters and headhunters are working with several jobs at a time, but for the sake of this explanation, let's consider that there is just one opening.
2) **A job description is written for that position based on the best possible understanding of the requirements.** Sometimes this is based on the previous person who did the job. Other times this is based on some job description that

was found on the Internet and then modified based on what the hiring manager wants for the role. It may also be based on a previous job description for the same role. On rare occasions, the job description is written from scratch for the role.

3) The company *may* **post the job online**. Frequently, the job posting goes up on the company's website. Sometimes, it will go out to job boards (Monster, Dice, CareerBuilder, LinkedIn, etc.) and classified style listings (like Craigslist). More and more companies are also using social media to post opportunities.

4) **The company may not post the position *anywhere*.** There are several cases where a job description might not get published online:

   a. It's a confidential position
   b. The position has been posted recently and there are already enough candidates in the candidate pool to be able to identify a good candidate
   c. The role will be filled by someone internally
   d. The role will be filled by someone externally who has already been identified
   e. Individuals within the company have a huge referral network to tap into
   f. The recruiters fear that they will be overwhelmed with a massive quantity of resumes
   g. The company can't afford to pay for an official posting and they don't have a place to post jobs on their website
   h. The system for posting jobs at a company does not give accurate visibility into the candidates who have applied for their jobs

5) **Sometimes a candidate is chosen before a position even gets posted.** The posted job may thus no longer be a "real" opening. However, the position may still be posted online in order to follow a set of processes and procedures. Employment law can sometimes come into play so that all applications are handled exactly the same way.

6) **Within 24 hours, a company normally receives more than 400 submissions for the posted position.** Because the job is posted online, people from all over the world may apply for that position. You may be applying for a position in Chicago, but competing with people from New York, London, Houston, or anywhere around the world.

7) **Job Seekers are applying for positions that are not suited for them.** Some job seekers do it because they are desperate to find ANY job. Some job seekers do it because they think they are playing a numbers game – if they can just apply to enough positions surely one will come through. Some job seekers do it because they MUST apply for a set number of positions in order to receive unemployment benefits. I have seen applications come through for a Network Engineer where the resume clearly indicates that that person has been a plumber for their entire career.

8) In order to filter through the pile of resumes received, there must be some process to whittle down the applicants. **Many companies have resorted to what are called "keyword searches."** This means that they have defined

some words that they believe are important for the role. Each resume is electronically scanned to see if the preset words appear in the resume. The system that scans for "Account Executive," may not select the resumes that only include "Account Manager."

9) **Companies begin a very selective process to whittle down the remaining applicants to a manageable set.** They might delete you from the pile if your resume does not include education information, even though you may have worked in a similar role as the open position for a significant amount of time. They might pull you from the pile because you have a typo. In order to get the pile to a reasonable size, the company must find reasons to rule people out rather than rule them in. It really doesn't matter why; they are looking for reasons to exclude you, not include you.

10) **Sometimes, the job requirements will change once a hiring manager starts to see what kinds of talent is available on the open market.** Most of the time, the online job description is not updated to reflect this change in requirements.

11) **Until a candidate gets a phone screen, they are simply ones and zeroes in a database, or possibly a piece of paper**. There may be several candidates who read the job description and feel that it was written for them. The person screening through the batch of resumes has to make a decision on who might be a better fit for the role simply based on what is written on the application or resume.

12) **Internal referrals take precedence**. While there are a number of online resumes that get submitted, the screener who receives a recommendation by an employee is far more inclined to include the referrals into their "selected" pile. Frequently, the internal referrals produce a large set of good potential candidates; therefore, the company does not need to look at the electronic submissions.

13) **The company then selects 3 - 10 people** out of the pile of resumes to send through the interview process. Unfortunately, because there are so many applications, there's no way for the company to go back and contact everyone who has applied for the position, unless an automated response process is part of the candidate database. Recruiters/headhunters will only go back to the pool if they determine that none of the 3 - 10 people are a fit for the role, or if they have multiple positions to fill.

14) **The job description does not come down from the website until the position has been filled**. Some companies will leave a position open indefinitely if they know that they will frequently be hiring for that position.

Many candidates who are a "perfect fit" for a role are never even pulled from the pile before the initial 3 - 10 candidates are identified. If there's a large pool to pull from, candidates will be dismissed from the selection process for any number of reasons.

Most recruiters/headhunters would love to have the opportunity to reach out to every single candidate who applies for every job they have and let them know whether or not they are a fit for the role. The reality is that MOST recruiters/headhunters do not have the time to contact every applicant. Frequently, when they do take the time to reject a candidate, they are faced with harsh reactions from the rejected candidate.

When I started recruiting, I wanted so badly to reach out to every single person who applied for my positions and at least give them closure if they were not a fit. However, the reality is when you are hiring for multiple different roles at a time, it takes all the time you have just to work with your top choices and get them through the process. There are some headhunters/recruiters who are able to respond back to every single person who applies for a job they have posted. This is the exception and not the rule. It cannot be counted on.

What happens after you click "Reply" makes your chances of being hired through an online application very small. While this may paint a very bleak picture, this workbook is designed to help you find alternative ways to be considered for a position. Along the way, I will also show you how to transition from looking for A JOB, to finding THE RIGHT JOB for you.

Tackling it from the Top

Many job seekers start their job search process by going online to a job board (like Monster, CareerBuilder, *etc.*) or a job board aggregator (like Indeed or Simply Hired) and they type in their job title. They scan the list of jobs available at that moment. When they find something they are interested in, they click on the link and review the description to see if they are a fit for the position. Once they determine that they are a fit, they then look at the company who has posted the position. Sometimes the company matters to the job seeker, and sometimes it doesn't.

Using this isolated approach severely limits your potential opportunities. You're only looking at the positions that are currently posted via the site that you are reviewing. You may have missed previously posted positions that have not yet been filled but are no longer posted. You may have missed something that has not been posted online. You may miss new opportunities that are still coming.

Not only is the system broken for the applicant, but it is broken for the employer. Many employers don't have the time to weed through the hundreds of resume submissions. Instead, they look to their personal network to find the best fits for the roles that need to be filled.

My approach suggests that you start by looking at what kinds of companies on which you'd like to focus. From there, you can hone in on the companies that you would be interested in working with. Accountability Groups and Daily Habits can help set you on the right track. If you aren't already an expert for the role you are seeking, discovery meetings can help you gain knowledge and build your network within your field of interest. Then, you need to go around the automated system and access the human system of interaction to find your new role at your target company.

While this is a lot more work than sitting at your laptop hitting Apply, Apply, Apply, it is guaranteed to produce better and faster results for a more fulfilling career. Those who take a different approach from the masses get better jobs than the masses.

When Job Boards Can Be Used For Good

I know you love the job boards. You love to search the lists trying to find companies that are hiring and looking just for you. It's so easy, right? You just find the job, hit Apply and attach your resume. Then you spend your days expecting someone will see your resume and get back to you. Remember, this works for only six percent of job seekers. Many people hear the success stories of this small group of people and pin all their hopes on the idea that they will win, too. You might as well start playing the lottery while you're at it. To top it off, many people who play this numbers game will play the game for months before they find any success. Since the odds are so poor, relying exclusively on job boards isn't a good strategy.

That being said, job boards (and their aggregator counterparts) are not ALL BAD.

1) Job boards give you an idea about companies that are currently hiring (even if they don't have a posted position that is a match for your skill set).
2) Job boards may help you to identify companies that you hadn't considered before.
3) Job boards can give you some insight into an organization that will give you something to talk about at a networking event

If you use job boards as your research tool – and not your lifeline – then you are using job boards effectively. Like I said, sometimes the Apply button works. However, this workbook is about identifying alternatives to the Apply button.

Now, let's start to look at this journey through another perspective.

Defining Your Company Categories

I would not suggest that anyone try to initiate a job search all by himself or herself. You should be using everyone around you to help you find your next position. Unfortunately, if you just tell them that you are looking for "a job," there's no place for them to start.

I'm sure that you don't want just ANY old job (although some days it might feel that way). For some reason, job seekers like to tell their friends and family about the job title that they are seeking. "Let me know if you see a finance position open up." Because people hear about that kind of thing every single day, right? Admittedly, sometimes it works. They could be in exactly the right place, at the right time, where someone brings up the position and they think of you to fill the role. Do you really want to play those odds? Personally, I like to give people bigger chances to help me be successful.

Consider these two statements:

"Hey John. It's been a long time since I've spoken with you. I hope that your family is doing well. I'm in the midst of a job transition right now. I'm looking for a position as a sales executive. Do you know anyone who might be hiring right now? "

Or

"Hey John. It's been a long time since I've spoken with you. I hope that your family is doing well. I'm in the midst of a job transition right now. I'm really interested in talking to companies who are doing something in the retail industry. Do you know anyone in that industry?"

Depending on who John is, he might have some ideas of people who are hiring for your job title at the moment. When you open it up to ANYONE who works in a particular industry your chances of success are much higher. Of course, you might be thinking; "I don't want just ANY job in that industry, I want a Sales Executive position in that industry." That comes later. At the beginning, you want to start with a greater number of options and then whittle them down as you get more information.

So, how do you start to identify which industries (or company groupings) you might like to work in? Consider these different ways to slice the list. (Multiple choices on any question are fine, and start answering the questions below.)

1) What size of company would you like to work in?
    a. 0 – 10 employees
    b. 11 – 50 employees
    c. 51 – 100 employees
    d. 101 – 500 employees
    e. 501 – 1,000 employees
    f. 1,000 + employees

2) What stage of growth would you like the company to be in?
    a. Development – Just an idea
    b. Introduction – Startup
    c. Growth
    d. Maturity
    e. Decline

3) What industries have you worked with in the past?

_____

_____

_____

4) What industries interest you?

_____

_____

_____

_____

_____

_____

If you are having trouble identifying a list of industries, do a search for "Industry List" or use a tool like LinkedIn.

LinkedIn is an online tool that allows you to build a personal profile by entering your professional information and search for contacts that you are connected to (either through networking or previous employment).LinkedIn has a search mechanism that allows you to search for companies based on industry.

Are there any other ways that you would like to slice up your list?

For example, I've had people tell me they want to work for a company that

- Is global
- Is doing something highly creative
- Contributes to humanitarian causes
- Is on the cutting edge of technology
- Does something to help animals

Use this space to add to your list anything else that you might consider:

_____

_____

_____

_____

_____

_____

_____

_____

Alternatives to the Apply Button

Now that you have taken some time to consider your options, pick eight company groupings/industries from above that you would like to focus in on. This list can change over time but you must start somewhere. Make sure that you can think of at least three companies that can be included in each grouping. If you want to stay in your current city, make sure there are at least three companies in that grouping in your city. Simply saying "Companies who are Hiring" does not count as a grouping.

Here are some examples that show you the difference between an Industry and a Grouping:

Industries
- Green energy
- Manufacturing
- Education
- Hospitality
- Retail
- Non-profits

Groupings

- Small business startups of less than 50 people
- Companies who work with governmental agencies
- Companies who deliver a creative product
- Women-owned businesses
- Global companies

Here's space to create your list of your top 8 Industries/Groupings:

1) _____

_____

2) _____

_____

3) _____

_____

4) _____
   _____

5) _____
   _____

6) _____
   _____

7) _____
   _____

8) _____
   _____

For the sake of clarity I'm going to refer to industry/groupings as your "Company Category" through the rest of this section. In order to make sure you have identified valid "Company Categories," list three companies that would fall in your defined categories from above. If you can't come up with all three right now, but you believe there are at least three in each city where you are looking for work, that's okay. If you can't come up with three, then you've defined your category too narrowly and you should broaden the category.

Be careful not to choose the category based on the companies that are in it. Instead, choose the category, and then fill in the companies.

I was working with an individual who really, really wanted to work at one particular company. She was so focused on that company that she stated her company category was "Online Vacation Rental Companies." In Austin, Texas (where I am), there's currently exactly one company that fits that bill. This was not going to be a valid company category if she wanted to stay in Austin. I suggested that she broaden her company to "Online Travel," "Travel Related Industry," and "Hospitality." Ultimately we got down to the real root of the category she was looking for, which she named, "Global Companies with an Online Product."

Based on the company categories that you've chosen above, identify three companies that meet your criteria.

Company Category 1	
Company 1	
Company 2	
Company 3	

Company Category 2	
Company 1	
Company 2	
Company 3	

Company Category 3	
Company 1	
Company 2	
Company 3	

Company Category 4	
Company 1	
Company 2	
Company 3	

Company Category 5	
Company 1	
Company 2	
Company 3	

Company Category 6	
Company 1	
Company 2	
Company 3	

Company Category 7	
Company 1	
Company 2	
Company 3	

Company Category 8	
Company 1	
Company 2	
Company 3	

It's essential that you define eight company categories that interest you when you are starting this process. In a moment, I'll ask you to choose your top three categories to provide a better focus for your efforts. Through the discovery process, you may realize that one (or more) of your categories no longer interests you. At that point you can easily pull another company category from your list to start tracking that one. Having eight to start with allows you to continue the job search process in another category when you get to a point where you feel you're not making enough progress in the categories you first chose.

Choosing Your Top 3 Company Categories

It's time to narrow the list from eight company categories to your top three company categories. When you review your list of Company Categories above, which of the three categories really excites or interests you? Which of these categories has the most potential to hire at the moment? Which of these categories do you already have insight and knowledge of? There should be something that will compel you to choose three from the list. If not, choose a random three and start from there.

Choose your Top Three now:

Company Category 1 _____

Company Category 2 _____

Company Category 3 _____

Remember that through the discovery process, you may choose to eliminate one of these categories and substitute in a new one. Just start the process over with the new category and keep moving. Movement is the key in a job search. You can't allow yourself to get stuck.

Creating a Top 10 Target List within Your Company Categories

You may have had trouble coming up with three companies for your company categories. If so, the next task may prove to be even more difficult. Your goal is to determine a list of your top ten companies within each of your top three company categories. If you already know your top ten target companies for a given category, then you can skip to the bottom of this section.

There are several online tools that you can use to help you to get a better understanding of companies within your chosen category. Friends and networking colleagues can also be essential allies in helping you to identify your list of target companies within each of your company categories.

Who Do You Know Who Has Some Knowledge About Companies In Your Company Category?

Salespeople are a great resource when it comes to companies in your top 3 categories. They are normally very approachable in an organization. They frequently have their own target company lists for a given space. They may also be able to identify vendors who support the space that you are looking into.

Even if you don't know a salesperson, you may know people who are already working in the category that you have identified. For example, if your category is "education," you might contact a professor that you had in college. If your category is "retail," you can easily walk into a retail store and ask for the general manager.

For each of your top 3 categories, see if you can identify five people that you can talk to who have some knowledge about which companies are part of your category. If you don't have five people, keep on the lookout for someone who might be a potential contact.

Company Category 1	
Contact #1	
Contact #2	
Contact #3	
Contact #4	
Contact #5	

Company Category 2	
Contact #1	
Contact #2	
Contact #3	
Contact #4	
Contact #5	

Company Category 3	
Contact #1	
Contact #2	
Contact #3	
Contact #4	
Contact #5	

What Networking Events In Your Town Cater To People Who Are Interested In Your Company Category?

In many cities, there are networking events for almost everything. In Austin, there are 400 organizations and associations and several thousand Meetup (www.meetup.com) groups. Most cities have a community calendar set up either through their newspaper or a local television station.

If you can't find networking groups that are actively meeting, try going out to LinkedIn and search for groups that cater to your identified company category. Post a discussion to the group asking to see if anyone is aware of a local group meeting to discuss the topic.

Creating Your Top 10 Companies List

Once you've identified resources that can help you to form your list of companies in your company category, you're ready to start to identify which companies are in your top 10 Companies list.

Depending on the category, you may discover that it's very easy to come up with your initial top 10 Companies OR you may struggle to come up with three companies who make the list. Your top 10 Companies list may change over time as you find out more information. Do not get discouraged; you will see your list build over time.

When you have ten companies on your target list for an industry, you can go to your contacts in the industry, or people at a networking event, and ask them if they happen to know anyone who works at the companies that you have identified. Ten companies is a manageable size from which to make a request. Too many companies and people feel overwhelmed. Too few companies limit your chance of success in finding a contact.

Alternatives to the Apply Button

Use the space below to see how many companies you can identify within your top 3 Company categories.

Company Category	
Company 1	
Company 2	
Company 3	
Company 4	
Company 5	
Company 6	
Company 7	
Company 8	
Company 9	
Company 10	

Company Category	
Company 1	
Company 2	
Company 3	
Company 4	
Company 5	
Company 6	
Company 7	
Company 8	
Company 9	
Company 10	

Company Category	
Company 1	
Company 2	
Company 3	
Company 4	
Company 5	
Company 6	
Company 7	
Company 8	
Company 9	
Company 10	

Do you have your five contacts per company category? Do you have your ten companies within that category? If you do, fantastic! If not, that's okay; you can start with what you have. It's time to reach out to your five contacts and ask them if they have anyone who can introduce you to the ten companies that you have listed.

If you are struggling to identify your companies and contacts, networking events are a great place to go to gather information. You can go to a networking event and ask:

- Who are the top 3 companies that you think of in <company category>?
- Who do you think is the best person you know who has some knowledge about <company category>?
- Do you know anyone work works for <company name>?
- Would you be willing to make an introduction to your contacts at <company name>?

At many networking events, people include their company name on their nametag, which helps to make your search even easier. You'll find more tips and techniques on networking, in my workbook, "Network Like a Pro: Building Valuable Contacts and Connections."

If meeting people at networking events scares you, you can start by sending out your target list of companies to everyone you know. You never know how one person might be connected to a company.

You might say something like:

Dear <Friend> -

I am looking to gather more information about <Company Grouping>. I find it interesting because <state the reason you picked the grouping>. I'm currently trying to find contacts that I can speak to within these companies:

- *Company 1*
- *Company 2*
- *Company 3*
- *Company 4*
- *Company 5*
- *Company 6*
- *Company 7*
- *Company 8*
- *Company 9*
- *Company 10*

If you know anyone who is currently working at one of the companies I listed, I would really appreciate an introduction.

Thank you so much for your help, <Your Name>

Finding Internal Champions

"Internal Champions" are the MOST important tool you can use in order to help you get introduced to an organization. Later in this workbook, I will share methods for finding internal champions within your target companies. For now, it's important to understand *why* internal champions are so important.

When you have an internal champion vouching for you within an organization, the entire job search process runs so much more smoothly. Your champion can go and figure out what is happening in the hiring process for you. If the process starts to get stuck your internal champion can help to remove the roadblocks in the way. Your internal champion helps you to get out of the black hole and uncovers real information for you during your job search process.

Internal champions alone cannot get the job for you. You still have to go through the interview process just like you would for any other job. However, they provide great power and leverage to help you move more seamlessly through the process.

Eighty percent of all jobs come from referrals. If you enter the hiring process through a referral, you suddenly go from being an unknown entity to a known entity. If you've worked with the person referring you, they will be able to attest to your ability to do the work. If they like you, they can attest to your ability to fit in with the company culture. Companies prefer the certainty of an internal referral compared to someone who they have simply met through the interview process. And when jobs are not posted publicly and people are simply hired based on asking other people at the company if they know anyone who is a fit for the job, an internal champion is the ONLY way you'll be considered at all.

Headhunters and Recruiters

Headhunters and recruiters can be a valuable tool in your toolset when looking for a job. Headhunters work for organizations or companies whose sole mission is to help outside companies find candidates for jobs. Recruiters are individuals who work within organizations or companies and are tasked with the responsibility of identifying candidates for an internal position.

The Headhunter's Mission

A headhunter is hired by an organization with the expectation that the headhunter will deliver three great candidates for an organization to choose from and interview. Occasionally, headhunters will be offered an exclusive contract with an organization. More frequently, hiring companies will contract on a non-exclusive basis with several headhunters to supply their three best candidates for a position. In order to get paid by the organization, the headhunter must supply the best possible candidates that they have in their roster at the time.

If you are one of the three best matches for a position, then you will receive a lot of attention from the headhunters. If you are not a fit for any of the positions that they are *currently* working on, then they really can't afford to spend a whole lot of time with you. This is not meant to reflect negatively on you, it's just the reality of what headhunters need to do in order to be successful in their job.

Working with Headhunters

Headhunters are constantly working on multiple job postings at a time. It is never clear when a match will occur. This is a benefit to job seekers, because, they may have several opportunities for the same position across a variety of different organizations. Headhunters normally have some sort of niche (Technology, Legal, Financial, Executive, *etc.*). If you can find a headhunter in your niche that you can trust, then you've got a really good tool on your hands.

Headhunters are always calling into organizations looking for the next deal. Talk to friends who are hiring managers in your functional area to see if they have been contacted by a headhunter that they like. Headhunters can come off as very pushy. If they are upsetting the hiring managers, then you don't want to work with those individuals. However, if you find one that hiring managers like, you have a good chance that they will have a lot of opportunities available.

When you find a headhunter that you like and trust, keep up with them. Most people believe that if they haven't heard from you in a month, then you have found a job. They will not be thinking of you when an opportunity comes up. Build a good relationship with that headhunter (go and meet them if you can) and contact them every few weeks to let them know that you are still on the market. When they find a fit, they will reach out to you.

Some headhunters are looking for leverage into an organization. If you are a strong enough candidate for a position, headhunters will be happy to present you to an organization. Frequently, they may forgo a fee for you this time, in order to ensure that they will have future business. Additionally, if you are in a position to be a hiring manager, the headhunter will look to you to use them when you are looking to hire someone in the future.

It's okay to work with multiple headhunters, but make sure that you stay on top of which headhunters are submitting you to which organizations. Organizations do not want to get involved in a "who collects the fee" scenario when they want to hire an individual. They want it to be very clear that you came from one particular source.

Headhunter fees are charged to a company after they hire you. These fees are established in advance with their clients. A headhunter should never charge a candidate a fee for helping them to find a job. Do note that some headhunters are also career coaches. Career coaching activity involves all the prep work that happens in advance of introducing you to companies and organizations. If a fee is requested be sure that you know what kinds of services are being offered.

The Apply button will work against you if you are using a headhunter. If you apply to a position online, this will rule out the headhunter's ability to work with you. Most organizations won't pay a fee for someone who has already come through the system in another manner. The headhunter will not be able to negotiate on your behalf anymore. In some cases, the battles over fees have made organizations rule out any candidate who is submitted by more than one source. Be very aware of how you are being presented to a company.

On the other hand, if a headhunter believes in you, they will use their relationship with an organization to get in and fight on your behalf. They will champion you through the organization. They will fight for you to get an interview. They will combat any concerns that an organization has. They will help you work out a strategy for negotiating compensation Headhunters can be valuable allies, if you find a good one.

The Recruiter's Mission

Depending on the size of a company and the number of positions they are hiring for, a recruiter may or may not have recruiting as their only job responsibility. Recruiters are hired by an organization to find top talent. They are contacted by a hiring manager and given a job description. Some recruiters are very good at identifying top talent, others are not. They must scan through all of the resumes that come in for a position and decide who will move forward and who will not. They are also tasked with the goal of presenting the hiring manager only with the top matches for the position.

Working with Recruiters

Recruiters are bombarded with people who are trying to get into an organization. I've heard some recruiters say that they have had to report candidates to the police for stalking. When times are hard, people get desperate, and you don't want to be one of those desperate job seekers.

Alternatives to the Apply Button

If you have a target company that you want to work for, the recruiter within that company can be one of your best friends if you build the relationship with care. They will know the moment a job is even being considered (long before it is posted).It is possible to get the inside track with a recruiter.

The key is to build a good relationship with the recruiter and to have a little patience for the process. If a position is already posted, the recruiter is probably already flooded with applicants. If you can get to know a recruiter before a position is posted then you will have a better chance of success.

You can easily burn a bridge with a recruiter. Since they hold the keys to the start of the hiring process, you want to tread very lightly with them. Don't be overly pushy. See if you can get a champion within the organization to make the introduction. Whenever they reach out to you, follow up immediately. Once a relationship is created, reach out to them monthly to see if there is anything on the horizon that might be a fit. You have to have a lot of patience with this process. **Do not make it your only strategy.** However, when it works, it works well.

Becoming Accountable

Now that we've started to identify some company categories and companies within them, it's time to start the daily process of your job search. Remember, you can't do this job search alone. You need to build a support group. The job search can be very overwhelming at times. Frequently, it's hard to stay on task. In a work environment, you have a boss or team who helps you set goals and gives you deadlines. The world is made up of procrastinators; we must be given a timeline in order to tell us when we need to start working on something.

Spouses and family members are TERRIBLE accountability partners. They bring an emotional component to an already overly emotional job search. They have their own agendas on when they think you should get something done. They are just as worried as you about how bills are going to get paid. They want everything done yesterday. Until human beings are able to travel through time, we can't go back to yesterday.

Every person who is going through a job search should have at least five IMPARTIAL people to help hold them accountable to their job search. Many people turn to career coaches in order to help hold them accountable. Anyone who will hold you accountable will work for this process.

I call this group of five impartial people an accountability group. To find your group of five people consider looking at:

- People you go to church with
- Previous bosses and mentors
- Former colleagues
- Other job seekers

The key is to find five people who you feel comfortable with discussing your job search process. You need to plan to talk to these people on a frequent basis (at least once a month but once a week is preferred). You should talk to at least one person from your accountability group each week (even if you don't meet with all of them on a weekly basis).

You do not have to meet with your group as a group; you can meet with them individually. Set up a regular meeting time with each person in your group. It could be in person or over the phone. Make sure the time is predictable and does not get reset for a later date. Delaying a meeting will only delay the time it takes for you to find your next job.

The accountability group:

- Holds you responsible for completing all of the actions that you promise to complete in the timeframe that you agree to complete them
- Listens to the challenges that you face in your job search and helps you identify solutions to those challenges
- Is a consistent part of your job search process so that they can celebrate the successes with you
- Meets with you in a repeatable, predictable time frame

I suggest that these meetings should be scheduled for 30 minutes to an hour. If you are combining more than one person in the group, then the timeframe should be extended appropriately.

If you find that an individual is not meeting your expectations, you should graciously thank them for their assistance and find another individual to be part of your group.

Who are your five people for your accountability group?

1) _____
2) _____
3) _____
4) _____
5) _____

If you'd like, you can create a pledge or contract between you and your accountability group partners. Here's an example:

I, (Job Seeker), pledge to work with (Accountability Partner) during my job search process. I understand that I need to be forthcoming and truthful throughout the process because I only hurt myself by doing otherwise. I promise to be on time and present for every meeting. I promise to accomplish all tasks that I have set out for myself before the next meeting. If I am unable to accomplish all of my tasks I understand that it will affect my ability to find a new job quickly. I understand that my accountability partner is doing this as a favor to me during this difficult time. I promise that should my accountability partner ever need me for their job search process, I will always be available to them.

I, (Accountability Partner), pledge to hold (Job Seeker) accountable during their job search process. I will respectfully point out any time where I feel the job seeker is not meeting their obligations to the accountability group. I promise to be on time and present for every meeting. I promise to listen to the job seeker and offer constructive solutions wherever I see them. I look forward to the moments where I can share the job seeker's successes. I know that, should I ever need help from the job seeker in the future for my own job search process, they will be there for me.

Of course, you can come up with your own contract or pledge. Note that I never made any indication that money would change hands in this process. If a financial obligation makes sense between you and your accountability partner (*i.e.*, you're working with a career coach), then feel free to work that into the contract or pledge. HOWEVER, you should not have to pay for any accountability partner to work with you. There are plenty of people who are happy to help you out of the goodness of their heart, with the understanding that you will help whenever you are able.

When you are working with your accountability group, you can use whatever format works well for you. Remember they are there to help you stay accountable to yourself and what you promise to do for yourself during your job search process. The key is to find someone who will listen to the steps that you are taking and help you to determine the next steps for you to take.

I suggest that you use a predefined format whenever you are working with an accountability partner. Here is the format I use:

Date of Meeting
Accountability Partner
Tasks that I committed to during our last meeting (completed items designated with a checkmark)
Wins and successes since our last meeting
Reasons why any tasks have remained uncompleted

Alternatives to the Apply Button

Challenges and obstacles since our last meeting

Possible solutions discussed during our meeting

Tasks that I commit to complete before our next meeting

Accountability partner action items (if any)

Next meeting time/date

Other notes

I've added a few of these templates to the end of the workbook to help you get started. Whenever I am part of an accountability group, I ask that the job seeker keep a working journal of each of these items in between meetings so that they will remember them as each element occurs. You want to give adequate time to celebrate the wins (no matter how little). You also want to make sure that you address any challenges, as they come up, so that they don't become a burden.

The Accountability Meeting is not an opportunity to complain. It is an opportunity to embrace the good things that you are doing for your job search, as well as find out how you can make the job search better by finding solutions to your challenges.

Setting Up Good Daily Habits

Most of us wouldn't think about letting a day go by without brushing our teeth, taking a shower or making meals for ourselves. Okay, maybe on the days we're stuck on the couch we don't actually shower, but don't go around telling other people about that.

Why is it that we don't set daily habits for our job search process? Establishing good daily habits can help us to do little things that end up making a great impact in our job search. The key to setting up a good daily job search habit is understanding why you're setting the habit for yourself in the first place.

For example, you might set a habit for "I will search the job boards for 15 minutes a day – no more, no less." Remember that some good things can happen by reviewing the job boards, but you don't want to make it a big part of your day because the success factor is so low.

Feel free to create whatever habit you'd like. I'll list some of my favorites (and their reasons) below. Choose ten that you will commit to doing every single day.

HABIT	REASON
I will reach out to one new person today and request a discovery meeting with them	The more discovery meetings (more on that below) you set up, the quicker your success in finding a job that you love.
I will follow up with anyone who I've met within the last two days	Follow up is essential in your job search process. Time kills all excitement, so the quicker you can get back to people the better. Even if they don't have an action item, it's still good to send out a "nice to meet you" email to build rapport.
I will find an hour to enjoy myself today	Many job seekers feel very guilty if they take any time to enjoy themselves, instead of working on their job search. Sometimes the guilt will spiral into getting you stuck and overwhelmed. If you allow yourself an hour to recharge your batteries and do something just for you, you'll be amazed at how much better you will feel. Find something that will help to de-stress you. Please note that enjoying yourself does not necessarily equal spending money, for those on a limited budget.

I will spend an hour researching companies in my company category	It's always good to do more research on companies that you are interested in. The more information you have, the more equipped you are to get out there and get a job at one. Research can frequently lead you down a rabbit hole and take all your time. So make sure that you put a limit on your time spend doing research.
I will make my bed and cook myself (and/or my family) breakfast every morning	I put this habit in as something that makes you feel "normal." It's good to have something in your habit list that you will continue to do even while you are working. This way you won't be out of the habit when you take on that shiny new job.
I will take a shower and leave the house at least once during the day	Even if you just drive down to the gas station and back, getting yourself cleaned up and out of the house does amazing things for your psyche. We've all had those days where we're still sitting around in our pajamas at 5:00 p.m. wondering where the day went.
I will take at least one action a week that helps someone else in my network. Examples: • Write a recommendation for someone on LinkedIn • Review a resume • Serve as an accountability partner	It's important to do something good for someone else. Job seekers need so much help during their job search that they frequently feel like takers instead of givers. Doing something that makes you feel like you are giving back can always be refreshing.

I have limited my list of daily habits to eight (yep, one was hidden in the intro) because I don't want you to "take my list" without putting thought into what is really going to work for you. Consider my reasons for choosing each habit and create your own habit list.

My Ten Daily Habits

	Habit	Reason
1		
2		
3		
4		
5		
6		

7	
8	
9	
10	

For the first 21 days (it takes 21 days to make a habit stick) start a spreadsheet, journal, or log book to track your ten daily habits and whether or not you actually did that item each day. You may find the job you are looking for within that time frame. If so, identify the habits that you are going to continue and keep the list going for a full 21 days. If you would like, you can use the log at the end of the workbook. If you find that you are not following that habit, explore why that is. Is it not a beneficial habit? If so, create a new one that is more important to you so that you will be motivated to practice the habit every day.

The Funnel Approach

Once you have decided the direction you'd like your career transition to head by defining your company categories, selecting your initial target list of companies, creating your accountability group, and establishing good daily habits, the next step is to identify the SPECIFIC companies that potentially are the best match for you.

When you're in the midst of a job search, you should always be looking at new companies that you match your company categories. Think of your job search as a process that narrows your focus until you reach the right goal, much as a funnel concentrates water.

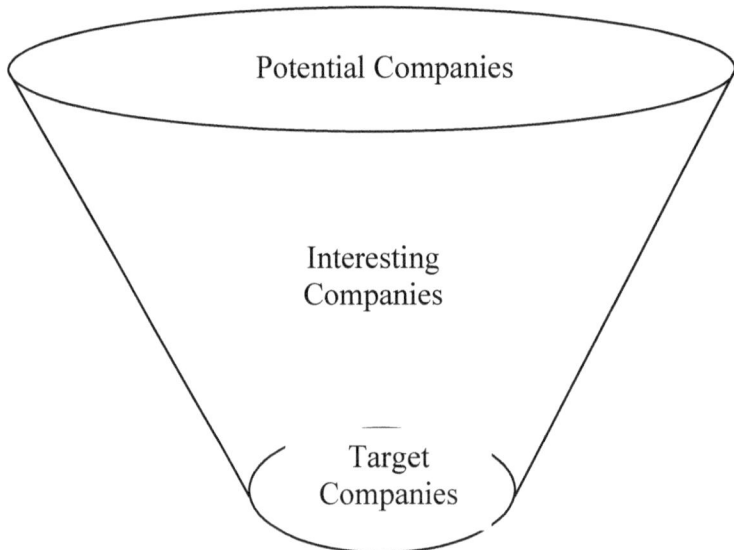

Every day you should be adding to your list of potential companies. You might hear an advertisement on the radio. You might spot a press release. Someone might mention a company name in passing. Jot down all of the companies that interest you. You can use those resources to go back and research if the company is one where interested in working. Take care not to become overloaded and overwhelmed by trying to research them all at once. Simply start the list so that you have new things in your funnel when your funnel starts to empty.

When you are starting your funnel for the very first time, you will want to build your interest list slowly so that you don't bite off more than you can chew. Work at the pace that is comfortable to you. Because you can't possibly research every company that you run across, start by defining which companies are on your Top 10 list in your Top 3 company categories. This becomes your "Interesting Companies" list. I suggest that you have no more than twenty companies on your list at any one time. If you have 10 companies in each of your three company categories, choose only twenty from your lists – thirty can be too overwhelming. The moment that one company no longer is of interest to you, that's when you pull a new company from your Potential Companies list – your Company Category lists – to your Interesting Companies list. Ultimately, you will have a "Target Company" list will include the five to 10 companies you have thoroughly researched, have the potential to hire you, and where you have an internal champion to help you land the RIGHT job.

While twenty companies are great for keeping your ears open and for research, it will overwhelm people if you ask them to help you with a list of twenty companies. Instead, clearly communicate your Target Company list with the people you've identifies to help you with your job search. Use these companies in the course of conversation with others. This list can change every week if you'd like. If another company starts to become very interesting to you, replace a company on your Target Company list with the new company. The company you remove from the list should go back to your Interesting Companies list for you to come back to it later.

Both the Interesting Companies list and the Target Company list are very fluid. They should constantly change over the course of your search as you continue researching opportunities.

Feel free to store your list in any format that makes sense to you. Take special care to keep good notes on the information that you find on these companies. Some people chose to use a paper notebook. Some people choose to use an Excel spreadsheet. Some people even get very sophisticated and start to use a CRM (Customer Relationship Management) system to keep up with their companies. CRMs are frequently used by sales teams to manage their pipeline. There are many free CRM solutions out there for you if you choose to use one. Just pick something that will work for you.

Now, we're going to see how many companies you can identify at this moment for each of the list types. Feel free to come back and add names as you work through this workbook.

Potential Companies (45)

Alternatives to the Apply Button

Interesting Companies (20)

Target Companies (10)

Identifying Contacts

Once you have placed a company on your Target Company list, you should start to search for contacts that can get you in front of hiring managers in that company. Sometimes you will already have a contact within that organization; this makes your search much easier. Frequently, you will not have a contact. So, the question becomes – how do you get a new contact?

The first thing you should do is to reach out to the people who you know to ask them to help you identify contacts within your focus companies. People are connected to others in the most unusual ways. Your best friend's child may be playing baseball with the child of someone who works for one of your target companies. Your cousin may be part of a running club that includes people you could be introduced to. Your real estate agent may have just sold a house to someone who works for one of your target companies.

Take a moment to consider people in your life who know a large number of people. These people will be the first you'll want to approach. Remember, though, that even people who are not well connected still know people. Also keep in mind that you should be selective in who you approach. You don't want to wear out your welcome by asking for too many favors.

List twelve people who you will reach out to the moment you have ten target companies identified to see if they can help you connect into those companies:

The next thing you should do is get out and meet new people. For tips and techniques on networking, see my workbook, "Network Like a Pro: Building Valuable Contacts and Connections."I'll speak briefly on the subject here.

In a room full of people, someone in that room may know someone at the company that you have identified as your focus company. Time and again, I will prove this point in a large group by asking someone randomly for a company they are currently targeting. I then ask anyone else in the room that might have a contact at that company to raise their hand. Every single time at least one hand goes up. I've even seen it happen with obscure companies with fewer than ten employees.

Whenever you're with a large number of people, come equipped with your list of target companies. Choose three companies from the list and after you've built a little rapport with an individual, ask if they know someone at one of those companies. Once you find three people willing to make an introduction on your behalf, cross the name of that company off the list and add one of your other target companies to the list you're using for that networking event.

It might not be natural to lead the conversation with your list of target companies. If you don't find an opportunity to introduce a target company, be sure to close up the conversation with a statement like:

"It was very nice to meet you. I've really enjoyed this conversation. I hope we get the chance to talk again soon. In the meantime, I'm currently working on getting some contacts at a few companies. Would you mind if I shared them with you to see if perhaps you might know someone at one of them?"

Alternatives to the Apply Button

If for some reason the conversation ends before you have an opportunity to make your request, be sure to take down their contact information and send a follow up email where you can make your request. Of course, always offer to assist them in any way that you can.

A couple of Do's and Don'ts:

- DON'T force someone to help you with your list
- DON'T expect someone to help you with your list
- DON'T interrupt a conversation in order to have your list heard
- DON'T start a conversation with a new person with your list

- DO thank everyone for their help even if they don't have a contact for you
- DO offer to help them to reach goals they might have
- DO go out of your way to thank the person if their lead results in a meeting/interview

LinkedIn

LinkedIn (www.linkedin.com) is one of the greatest tools currently available to help people to find old colleagues and make professional business connections. Because LinkedIn is such an important tool, I am going to devote a portion of this workbook discussing the tool and how to use it.

When LinkedIn initially launched their tool, most people used the tool in order to make connections to help them find their next job. For a short period of time, being on LinkedIn meant that you were interested in making a career transition. This slowed the adoption of the tool.

In the last few years, LinkedIn has become a major social networking tool for professionals. LinkedIn is valued in many ways beyond just helping you to make the right connections into your next job. It is now widely accepted as the best resource for making professional connections.

LinkedIn can be very effective for you IF you learn how to use it correctly. However, using LinkedIn incorrectly has the potential to burn bridges. I discuss those pitfalls later in this workbook.

For those of you who are hearing about LinkedIn for the very first time, here's the high level overview. LinkedIn allows you to create an online profile that includes your previous work experience, associations, education, causes, and references. You can showcase your professional accomplishments using your online profile.

Once you have created your profile, you can reconnect with people who you worked with in the past. You can also import your contact list to find other contacts you might have that are currently on LinkedIn. LinkedIn can connect to your mail or Hotmail account to pull potential contacts. You can also export your contacts from Outlook and import them into LinkedIn to make it easier to reconnect with the friends already in your contact list.

Once you start to make connections, LinkedIn will tell you how your connections are connected to other people. For example, you connect to your neighbor, Bob. Bob has you as a contact as well as all the other people that Bob knows. LinkedIn gives you visibility into the people that Bob has already chosen to connect with. For example, let's say that Bob plays golf with Larry. You immediately have visibility into the people that Larry knows as soon as you connect with Bob, because Larry's connections are 2nd level connections for Bob. Each of Larry's connections is a 3rd level connection to you. You won't know which of Bob's connections that connects you, but you will know that one of Bob's contacts connects you to that 3rd level connection. You can ask Bob to connect you with his contact who knows the 3rd level connection you are targeting. Bob introduces you to Larry, who can directly introduce you to his contact.

Your LinkedIn Profile

Your LinkedIn Profile is used to help people to find you. You may find your next job by reconnecting with a former coworker who has a perfect opportunity for you. Recruiters are using LinkedIn more and more to find high quality talent. They do keyword searches all the time to find the individuals that they want to target. Your profile is the first piece that you need for effective use of LinkedIn in your job search.

Things to consider when setting up your profile:

- Is it robust?
- Does it include keywords?
- Does it look professional?
- Do you have recommendations?
- Who are your connections?

Is It Robust?

Recruiters want to find out as much information about you as they can before they pick up the phone and try to talk to you. Make sure that all of your job experience is filled out and complete. If you don't have a lot to say, take pieces from your resume and directly paste them in for each Job Experience section.

Having a robust profile also allows people to identify you as a former colleague (especially if you worked in a large organization and you have a common name).

Does It Include Keywords?

Recruiters aren't going to find you if they can't get to you through a common keyword. Make sure that your profile contains the keywords necessary to fill your role somewhere on your profile. If you don't know what those are, find other individuals who do what you do and see what they have on their profile.

Try doing a "People Search" in LinkedIn and use a keyword that you think would describe you. If it's a common keyword, you might want to filter by location. Look to see how far someone would have to go down the list to find you. Try this with a variety of different keywords to see where you show up.

Choose twelve keywords that you think would result in someone finding you through a keyword search:

Review the profiles of people at the top of the list when you enter your keywords. Why are they at the top of the list? What can you do to improve your ranking on the list? Your goal should be to show up in the top ten percent of the search (or the top 100 people) when looking at keywords that define you.

For example, I just did a search for PMP in Austin, Texas. It came back with a list of 1881 people. LinkedIn will not allow you to see more than the first 100 people in a search without paying for the premium service. If you are a PMP, you want to make sure that you come up in the top 100 when sorting by relevance.

Does It Look Professional?

Make sure that your LinkedIn profile looks professional. If you have typos or grammatical errors, you may never know that you were rejected for a job opportunity.

Frequently, I suggest that job seekers take their LinkedIn profile and copy it into Microsoft Word. That lets you see any typos or grammatical errors rather quickly. Make sure that you also find other people to review your profile on your behalf to ensure that what you have said makes sense to someone other than yourself. This is also a great activity to help you practice the habit of helping others.

Many people ask me if they should include their picture on their LinkedIn profile. My answer is "ABSOLUTELY."However, be sure to use a profile picture that looks professional. This is not the time to include a picture of your child, dog or favorite football team on your profile. People will use your picture to remind them whether or not they know you. Not everyone remembers people by name; and having a face to go with a name is a big help.

Some people are concerned that their picture will tell people how old/young they are. There are lots of ways to tell how old/young you are based on your education and work history. Also, if they intend to hire you, they will eventually meet you face to face. If they are going to rule you out based on how old/young you look, then it's better to get it over at the beginning.

Do You Have Recommendations?

Since LinkedIn encourages users to write recommendations for their contacts, of course people are going to look at your recommendations as research you. They will read what people say and look for a consistent theme. What most people don't consider is that while a recruiter is researching your recommendations, they will also research what you have said about other people. They will look to see if you can communicate professionally. They will look to see if you have taken the time to carefully make a recommendation or if you have just used a cookie-cutter and made the same recommendation for everyone you know.

Many people ask me about the whole "trading a recommendation for a recommendation" deal. This can easily be seen by someone writing a recommendation for you on June 7th and you recommend them on June 8th. This is very frequent behavior. Personally, I don't see anything wrong with it as long as both recommendations are well thought out. If someone takes the time to write a good recommendation for you, it really doesn't matter how it came to be.

You can always decide not to accept a recommendation that someone has written on your behalf. However, I would suggest that you not ask someone to rewrite a recommendation unless there are glaring errors in it. Every person has their own tone and style in writing. Requesting that they reword something might take away from the individual's tone and therefore the genuine sentiment.

Many people ask me about how many recommendations they should have. I don't know that there are a set number of recommendations. Five well-written recommendations will trump twenty poorly written recommendations every single time. So, get as many well-written recommendations as you can, but don't worry about the number.

Who Are Your Connections?

Take care in deciding whom you are going to connect to via LinkedIn. Make sure that everyone that you are connected to is someone that you know. How strong that relationship should be is a decision you can make on your own, just make sure that you do in fact know them.

For example, let's say that Jane is a recruiter for a big consulting group. Jane needs to hire a new Senior Manager. As Jane is looking through her contacts, she runs across Joe. Joe looks like an ideal candidate based on his LinkedIn profile. Jane can see that Joe is a 2nd level connection to her. Upon review, Jane finds out that their mutual connection is Steve.

Jane reaches out to Steve to find out information about Joe. If Steve comes back and gives Joe a glowing review, then Joe has just leap frogged to the top of the list. However, if Steve comes back and says: "Well, I don't really know Joe. I picked up Joe's business card at a networking event and then I added him as one of my contacts." All of a sudden both Steve and Joe's connections have lost substantial value. Steve can't tell Jane anything relevant about Joe. Jane can't trust that any of her other connections to Joe are valid. In fact, this may have just put Joe down on the bottom of the list of potential candidates. It's also a poor reflection on Steve.

Remember that if recruiters have a huge list of people to choose from, once they have found you, they will be looking for ways to rule you out, not rule you in.

Connecting to Contacts

LinkedIn gives you the ability to add contacts to your network. **You should only add contacts to your LinkedIn network if you actually know the person and you know that they would be willing to help you connect to other people.**

DO NOT
- Add someone to your network as a ploy to start a conversation
- Add someone to your network that you do not already know
- Try to sell someone something via adding someone to your network

Not everyone will be angry with you for breaking those rules. However, you can be sure that at least 85 percent of people that treat this way will be angry with you for trying. LinkedIn is not a popularity contest. No one wins for having the most contacts if those contacts provide no value by enhancing the professional network.

People hold their personal contacts in high regard. If you try to "break into" their contacts using a sales tactic, you have just blown your opportunity for getting a response.

LinkedIn has a default message when connecting to an individual - "I'd like to add you to my professional network on LinkedIn." Whenever you are connecting to an individual, you should change the default message to something to allow the person to remember where they know you from and why they would want to connect to you.

Consider something like:

Hello Alexander –

My name is Kim Brushaber. We recently met at a Social Media Club event. We talked about our mutual passion for wine.

I would like to add you to my network. Please let me know if any of my contacts can be of any help to you.

Thanks!

Kim

In this message, you are reminding the person where you met and what you talked about. You are also offering them the ability to help them as well.

Many people do not check their LinkedIn Profile on a regular basis. Reminding someone of how you know them will increase the chances of their accepting your invitation to connect.

Here's another example of a request to connect:

Hello Michelle–

It's been a long time since we worked together on the Customer Service Team at Wonderworld. I think it would be great if we could have the chance to catch up. It looks like you've taken some brave new steps in your career. I think we should connect so that I can keep better track of what you're doing in the future.

Thanks!

Kim

Be sure to keep your requests professional.

Schizophrenic (or Career Hoarding) LinkedIn Profiles

Frequently I talk to job seekers who have worked in a variety of different roles. Any of these roles are things that they would consider doing again. When in the midst of a job search, most people prefer to keep their options open so that can consider taking on a variety of roles. For example, they might be a fit for a Project Manager Role, a Business Analyst role or a Training role. For each of the roles, they would want to highlight different parts of their skill set.

When you applying for a position, you can create a highly customized resume for that position, highlighting why you are good for that one particular role. In fact, that's the best way to do it. However, with LinkedIn you only have one profile, so you should carefully consider how you want to portray yourself.

My general rule of thumb is to think of yourself as a tree. There is a root system consisting of all of your jobs that has built the foundation of where you have come to today. You have branches that extend up that could represent any number of possibilities for where your career could go. At the center of all of this, you have a trunk. This trunk is the core and essence of who you are today. In order to show that you are a solid stable tree, you must define your trunk. Unlike natural trees, this trunk can change over time. Whenever you evolve your core, you need to update your profile.

Let's define your trunk. You can come back to this section and play with it as much as you want.

Alternatives to the Apply Button

Start by asking yourself these questions:

- What is the general theme that has developed through my career?
- What have I enjoyed the most out of all the things I have done?
- If I could work just one role for the rest of my life, how would I define it?
- What is the one thing that I can always be counted on to do?
- What role will make me want to get up and get out of bed every day with a smile on my face?

Think about other questions that will help you get to the essence of what you want to do regardless of the role that you end up in – who you are professionally.
I looked back over the course of my career and realized that no matter what role I have taken on, I have always stood in a place where someone had a problem. Many times, they weren't even able to define that problem. I have helped them to get a better understanding of what the problem was, so that everyone involved could help to resolve it. I then came up with a variety of creative solutions that would help them past their problem.

It took me a long time to figure this out about myself. I'm not suggesting that you should be able to define the consistent trend throughout your career at this moment unless you've already spent a lot of time thinking about it. However, that should be your end goal. Ultimately, you want to be very clear and very solid on what your trunk – your core – is

Below, see if you can come up with a general concept of what your trunk (your core) might be.

Next, you can start to define what are all the roots and foundations that support your core. Look back over the course of your career and all the positions that you have held and see if you can identify the activities that you engaged in that support your trunk.

Alternatives to the Apply Button

Here's some space for you to do that for your last five positions. Feel free to take a notebook to draw your roots out for any other positions you might have held.

Position:
Supporting Functions:

Position:
Supporting Functions:

Position:
Supporting Functions:

Position:

Supporting Functions:

Position:

Supporting Functions:

Now that you have your roots defined, be sure to take those functions and make sure that they appear within the statements that you make about those positions on your LinkedIn profile.

Branches represent where your foundation – your roots – can take you next. Defining the branches is a little more difficult because your trunk can lead you off into a variety of different career paths. The way I have defined myself, I could be a social worker, a teacher, a consultant, a customer support rep, a diplomat, or pretty much just about anything. In order to come back to the center, I have to define just a few branches that are the ones that I am most interested in. I would suggest that you focus on five or less.

Your five favorite branches are:

| |
| |
| |
| |
| |

You can choose to switch to different branches at any point in time. All you have to do is go in and revise your profile.

Once you have set your trunk and your roots into your profile go back and review each of your job experiences to see if you can see your five branches within the statements that you have made. If you don't see a branch reflected in your profile, add a little leaf – a side note – to your profile that points out how that position applies to that branch.

For example, let's say I wanted to make Event Planner as one of my branches. I've worked in a lot of technical roles in the past. The functions that were part of my every day job had little to do with event planning specifically, although there are strengths that cross the borders of both (like managing schedules and organizing big groups of people). I might consider adding a leaf to a technical role beneath the functions like the following:

In regards to my interest in event planning, while I was in this role I helped plan the Christmas Party for 150 employees that, which included decisions regarding décor, catering and activities.

It's a step out from my every day role, but it highlights that I did have some activities regarding my desire to become an event planner. If people aren't interested in what I do along the lines of event planning, then they can skip over that sentence.

What leaves might you consider adding to your last five functions to support your branches?

Position:
Side notes:

Alternatives to the Apply Button

Position:

Side notes:

Position:

Side notes:

Position:

Side notes:

Position:
Side notes:

Position:
Side notes:

If you are going to add in these little leaves, take special care to explain why you are doing it in the header section of your profile. Note what your core strength (trunk) is and what your branches are and WHY you chose the branches that you did. Be sure to communicate that you would enjoy an opportunity working with any of your branches. You want to make sure people know you are serious about taking on the role that you are given and that you won't get bored and take off to another position later.

Remember that you do not have to have five branches; you may only have two branches. The idea here is to communicate what you have done and how that relates to what you want to do in a way that doesn't look too scattered.

Identifying Companies Using LinkedIn

LinkedIn is a great way to start to identify companies that you might like to target. As more and more people join LinkedIn, you have greater access to information regarding companies and individuals who work there.

Company Search

Company searches will allow you to be able to grow or shrink your lists in a variety of different ways.

You can do a **Keyword Search**. If the word is listed in the company description anywhere, then it the company will be returned in the list, sorted by relevance. This is the same process that you use when doing a People Search.

LinkedIn has a long list of Industries. You can refine your list of companies by setting up an **Industry Search**. Once you have chosen an industry, you can also define it by sub categories as well. Your Company Categories may be organized by Industry. If so, the Industry Search feature will be very productive.

You can do a **Location Search**. This will allow you refine the list to companies that are located in a particular area. It will return results if there are any people listed as being in that location and working for that company. You can further refine it by being headquartered in a location if you'd like.

You can limit a search based on **your connections** into a particular company. This will allow you to get a list of which companies are associated to you either on a 1st or 2nd degree connection.

You can limit your search based on **company size**. This is set by the person who creates (or maintains) the company profile. It is not uncommon for a number to be set and see more connections on LinkedIn than the number suggests. This simply means that no one has updated the profile since the company has grown. This is actually pretty normal for a smaller company.

You can limit based on companies who are **hiring**. The problem with this is that it will only return those who have decided to post a job via LinkedIn. LinkedIn used to provide job posting as a free service, but it doesn't any longer. You are still better off looking for companies who are hiring using a tool specifically designed for job postings, such as Job Board Aggregator. If a company has posted a job via LinkedIn, using the Hiring Search will help you to quickly find connections that can help you be considered for that position.

Company Profile

The Company Profile is full of helpful information.

Description – Each company profile includes the description of the company.

Follow Company – This is a new feature within LinkedIn. If you choose to follow a company you will get all of the LinkedIn updates pertaining to this company. Do be aware that you will be listed as someone who is following the company, so if you want to anonymously follow the company, do NOT use this feature.

Specialties – A company can list the specialties associated to their business. This is a good place to identify some company keywords.

Current Employees – This will help you to identify people who you know who currently work for the company. It will sort it based on their degree of separation from you.

Related Companies –This section is helpful because you can see any acquisitions that the company has participated in. You can also tell where the majority of people came from before they worked at the company and where they left afterwards. This will help you to create a list of related companies to the one that you are reviewing. There is also a section on who most of the employees are connected to, which will also give you a hint of related companies in the industry.

New Hires – This is a list of the newest hires to the company. If you are looking for information on what the hiring process is like, these people will be your best resources because they just went through the process. New Hires will also tell you how recently they were hired and who you have in common. The other way that New Hires become helpful is that you can see what position a new employee just left. If the new hire holds the same title as you, and has recently joined the company, it is quite possible that their position at the old company may still be available.

Former Employees – This will tell you the most recent departures from a company based on level of connection. Former employees are a great resource in telling you the ugly little secrets about a company. You can find out why they left and what made them decide to move to another company. Additionally, this is a great way to identify a potential hole in a company as well. If the departure was on good terms, a former employee may even be willing to refer you into their old position (if it has not been filled yet).

Recent Promotions and Changes – This is pulled whenever someone makes a title update within an organization. If you have friends who have been promoted at an organization that you are interested in working for, it's a great excuse to reach out to them and congratulate them on the move. This is also a great place to watch for your job title to see if someone has moved from your title to another part of the organization, revealing another possible hiring need.

Popular Profiles – This tells you who are the people who come up the most frequently in searches via LinkedIn within this organization.

Key Statistics – This will tell you where the majority of people are located (based on LinkedIn's data). It will give you headquarters info, industry info, what type of company, the company size, when it was founded, the website, common job titles, top schools, median age, median tenure and gender ratio of employees.

Recent Activity - This is what you get when you follow a company. It's just the most recent information on changes to people's profiles that work for an organization.

Jobs – If the company has posted jobs on LinkedIn, they will show up in this section.

News – This will give you any recent public news articles about the company.

Stock Information –If it is a publicly traded company, the LinkedIn Company Profile will provide stock information.

Skillset Search

A skillset search is a very specific way to do a keyword search.

For example, if you are a Java Programmer and you want to find out companies who are working with the Java Platform then you can do both a company keyword search and a people keyword search to see which companies come back with those results. You will have to drill into these profiles to make sure that it truly is a match. By typing in "Java" you may get some false positives, like coffee shops.

Let's say that you work in Marketing. You can quickly tell how big a company's marketing team is by doing a people keyword search with the term marketing in it. If it returns a lot of results, then you know that they have a large marketing department. A small result may indicate a small department OR it may indicate that many people at the organization have not yet added their profiles on LinkedIn.

By default, the keyword search will return results based on anyone who has ever worked for that company. You can refine it by choosing current employees or former employees if you'd like.

Skillset searches are a great way to help you to identify additional companies that you may consider adding to your Interesting Companies list.

Identifying Contacts within a Company

LinkedIn has three different levels of connection:

Level 1 - This is a person that you are directly connected to.

Level 2 – This is a person who knows a person that you are directly contacted to.

Level 3 – This is a person who knows a person who is connected to a person who is directly connected to you (two degrees of separation in the middle).

LinkedIn also has a designation of "Group"-" In this case, you do not have one of the above levels of connection, but you and the person you want to connect with belong to one of the same LinkedIn Groups.

If you are connected to someone at any of these four levels, those individuals will be returned to you via any search. Basic Searches will only return the first 100 results (you must upgrade your service to get more results).

You may also get results for people with whom you are not connected. In those cases, you'll see only the name (or sometimes just the job title) within the organization.

In order to initiate this search, simply do a People Search with the name of the Company that you are researching.

Searching for your own Job Title

Searching for your own job title is a great way to find out whether or not your role is currently filled in the company.

For example, if it's a small company they may only have C-Level personnel. If you are used to being a Director or a VP-level contributor then you may want to watch this company as it grows so that you can step into the role.

Another example is if you are a VP of Marketing, some organizations will allow a VP of Sales to run the Marketing team until it reaches a particular stage of growth. If you see a VP of Sales within a company but not a VP of Marketing then it might be worth it for you to start a conversation with the company in case they may need you in the near future.

Another example is if you are a Project Manager you may do a search on a company and find out that they have hired a dozen project managers. This will tell you that the organization values the role of project manager. It might be an opportunity for you to step in and fill that role for the organization.

If you do find your job title within an organization, you can review the other people who are currently working in that role and see what your competition is like. You may also consider reaching out to that person. If they are happy within the organization, then they may be willing to refer headhunters who contact them to you because they are unwilling to leave the company. If they are not happy within the organization, then it's possible that they may refer you as a possible replacement when they are looking to leave an organization.

Looking for the Gaps

Identifying gaps within an organization is a great way to find a new position. People frequently talk about the hidden job market. This is when an organization has a need for a role but they haven't published it anywhere.

If you do a search for your role and it isn't there, it might be a good opportunity for you to convince someone to bring you on board.

You can also use LinkedIn to track people as they move from company to company. If someone moves to another company, there's a good chance that their role may be open. Sometimes companies will choose to fill that role and sometimes they won't. It's a great opportunity for you to go in and present your case to the organization.

LinkedIn has the capability to show you Recent Hires and Former Employees to make identifying the possible gaps a little easier. To enhance this, you can do a job title search for your role to see who might be in the position currently.

LinkedIn Job Postings

LinkedIn has the capability for organizations to post jobs. This used to be a free service. They are now charging a fee. Some recruiters are seeing good success from this. It allows them to see who might be a good fit within their own referral network.

As a job seeker, you have visibility into how your contacts might be able to help you get into this new role.

I expect to see this functionality used a lot more in the future as recruiters continue to have piles of resumes dumped on them. It allows them to pick the people they want rather than sorting through a bunch of people who are not a fit.

Introductions through LinkedIn

Within LinkedIn, you have the ability to get introduced to five connections. You can use the 5 introductions with 2nd level or 3rd level connections. If at all possible, you should pick 2nd level connections because the closer the connection, the greater influence you will have. Of course, it's always better to use regular old email. However, sometimes people ask that you create an introduction on LinkedIn. This will allow someone to easily forward your request from you to one of their contacts.

If you find that the connection stalls via your friend remind your friend that you have an outstanding connection. If it stalls via the person you are connecting to, see if your friend would be willing to give the connection a little nudge on your behalf. Remember that you are asking your friend for a favor and you should always be polite. You can always withdraw a request for an introduction if you find that it has stalled or lingered for too long.

Make the introduction very easy on your friend. Be sure to convey your message with enthusiasm so that you can show them that it would be a great idea to interact with you.

You should also trust that if your contact says that it's not a good connection for you, then it's not. I have over 1,000 contacts. I'm not going to forward every introduction that comes my way. I know that some of my contacts are far too busy to be answering emails from people. Trust that your contact will be able to help you in the connection process, and is not trying to alienate you from the individual.

If you are connected via multiple friends – start with the ones that you know best first. Don't stop until you've made a solid connection to the person you wish to talk to. Imagine if that person comes to their desk and has eight people who all say that they should be talking to you.

Here's an example of a request for an introduction that you might send to someone in your contact's network:

> Hey Jason –
>
> LinkedIn says that you know Nicolas at Wonderworld. Do you think that he would be nice enough to have a conversation with me? I came across a posted position for Wonderworld that I am very interested in and I would like to gather some more information from him. Would you mind forwarding this introduction on my behalf?
>
> Thanks!
>
> Kim

Make sure that the request to your friend remains professional. It may get accidentally forwarded on along the way.

Alternatives to the Apply Button

You can also make a direct request to the connection within LinkedIn. Here's a draft:

> *Hello Nicolas –*
>
> *LinkedIn has shown me that we have multiple mutual friends. I have asked them to make an introduction to you on my behalf. I recently saw a job posting for a Marketing and Community Manager position. I think I am perfect for that role since I have many years' experience managing an online community for my church.*
>
> *Would you mind talking to me for 15 minutes so that I can get more information on what this position entails? I would like to make sure that we both feel that I am a fit for this position before I take up too much of your time. I know that your time is valuable and I'm sure that the hiring process is very time consuming for you.*
>
> *Please feel free to review my LinkedIn profile so that you can see a summary of some of my qualifications.*
>
> *I look forward to talking to you more about Wonderland and the posted position soon.*
>
> *Thanks!*
>
> *Kim Brushaber*
> *512-555-5555*

If you are forwarding an introduction on behalf of someone else, make sure that you indicate why you are forwarding on that introduction. Your contact will thank you for it.

> *Hello Nicolas –*
>
> *I'm forwarding on an introduction request on behalf of my friend, Kim. We worked together for several years. She is an amazing Web Developer. I'm actually surprised to see that she's still on the market.*
>
> *If you could help her out at all, I would really appreciate it.*
>
> *Thanks!*
>
> *Jason*

Take special care to be professional every time you communicate via LinkedIn.

I was once part of a 3rd degree connection request that could have gone very badly. My friend Eric from college wanted to connect to my friend Alex from college. Eric was new to LinkedIn and didn't have a lot of connections set up yet. When he tried to connect to Alex he saw that Alex was a 3rd level connection via another college friend, Matt. Because of the nature of 3rd level connections, Eric could not see that I was the point in between Matt and Alex. Eric was connected to Matt. Matt was connected to me. I was connected to Alex.

Eric wrote a very nice note to Alex about how it had been a long time since college and that he wanted to connect back up. Eric's comment to Matt (remember there is an email to the end person and an email to your connection) was a highly unprofessional rant about how stupid LinkedIn was and how he was furious that he couldn't connect directly to Alex. The email contained lots of profanities and suggestions on what LinkedIn might go do with itself.

In LinkedIn, you must explicitly delete the comment that the first person makes in order for the next person not to see it. Matt didn't do this. He sent me this scathing email with a note that simply said "Seems pretty harmless to me. Mind making the connection?" Matt knew that I knew Eric and it was a clear indication that Eric's hot-headedness had not changed since college. I knew that Alex probably wouldn't mind if I sent along the connection. Besides, Alex didn't have to respond back to the introduction. In this particular scenario everyone knew each other, and no harm was done. However, I really wanted to go back and write Eric and teach him proper etiquette for LinkedIn introductions.

All in all, I'm thankful because it gave me the perfect example of what not to do. Eric had no way of knowing that I was the connection in the middle. His comments could have kept him from making the connection to Alex that he wanted. It could have also burned a bridge with me.

Use this as a lesson to always maintain a professional tone when communicating via LinkedIn.

Using the InMail Feature of LinkedIn

LinkedIn has functionality that allows you to send email via LinkedIn. LinkedIn will charge you to send emails to random strangers. However, if you are part of a group, you can choose to allow other people in the group to contact you via InMail (you can also send messages to any of your contacts). This allows you to send InMail free of charge.

Personally, I don't think that you should ever send email via LinkedIn if you have to pay for it. I think there are much more valuable ways to be able to contact someone. LinkedIn InMail is not checked as frequently as a person's desktop mail. However, the option is available to you should you choose to upgrade your membership.

If you are going to send LinkedIn InMail, make sure that you maintain a professional tone and don't try to sell someone on something they don't want. It will just burn a bridge before you have the chance to build it.

LinkedIn Groups

LinkedIn has a variety of different groups that you can be a part of as well. Articles, announcements, and questions are posted within groups that you might not see if you are not part of the group.

One strategy is to find the individuals who work in a particular organization or job title and find out which groups they belong to. If there's no barrier to entry, you can always request to be part of that group.

Another strategy is to do a Group Search and find groups dedicated to a topic that you are interested in contributing to. That way, whenever a question is posed to the group, you can respond and quickly become known as an expert.

People who belong to a Group can post job openings free of charge to other members of the group. This is another great place to find opportunities that you may not have been aware of otherwise.

LinkedIn Answers

LinkedIn Answers is a great piece of functionality that few people take advantage of. In general, LinkedIn gives everyone the opportunity to post a question out to the entire LinkedIn Community. When you create a question, you can choose whether you want it to be publicly available.

For a job seeker, LinkedIn Answers can be valuable both from the perspective of asking a question and answering one.

LinkedIn Answers are a great way to tell people that you are interested in a particular topic of conversation. LinkedIn Answers can be sorted out into topics, or you can do a keyword search to find an interesting conversation that you would like to join.

List five topics areas where you have expertise:

Do an industry/keyword search within LinkedIn Answers to see if anyone is currently having a conversation on that topic. If you find question, see if it is something that you can answer. If it is, then go ahead and respond. When the time period ends for responses to the question (normally two weeks, but it can be set to anything), the person who asked the question will select someone as providing the "Best Answer."

Any questions where you have provided the "Best Answer" will show up on your LinkedIn profile and you will start to be showcased as the expert on that topic. It will help to build your credibility in your areas of expertise.

If you can provide answers to a few questions a week your credibility on that topic will quickly grow. You never know who might be out there reading your responses. This is also a great way to help to keep your skills fresh.

You can always ask questions as well. Questions you ask show up on your LinkedIn profile. If you have a particular area of research that you are interested in, use LinkedIn Answers to see if you can get feedback to help you with your case.

Recently, I was trying to find someone for an Account Executive position. My client was having a hard time finding people who were natural cold callers. So, I asked a question using LinkedIn Answers to see, "What's so hard about cold calling?" Within the responses, I found lots of natural cold callers who wanted to help people who didn't have that natural talent. If one of them been in the right location for the job, I would have interviewed them on the spot (that was my original intention, even though I didn't pose the question that way).I didn't find the right candidate, but what I ended up learning was so much more valuable. I got information on how to identify a natural cold caller as well as tips on training someone who does not have cold calling as a natural behavior.

You never know WHY someone is asking a LinkedIn question; it could quite possibly lead you to your next job.

Beyond LinkedIn

Sometimes you don't know that your perfect company is out there until you do a little research. Many job seekers simply look for the open jobs and then go out and apply. Your job is where you spend most of your waking hours; you should have a choice in where you are spending that time. You need to understand as much as you can about a company rather than just seeing what happens when you show up for your first day on the job.

While LinkedIn is an essential tool in your job search process, it is not the only place for you to identify companies that you might add to your Interesting Companies list. It certainly is not the only place for you to research a company. When you do get to a point where you are honing in on your set of target companies, you should spend some time doing additional research on the company so that you can be certain it is a company that you'd like to work with.

Of course, networking can help you to find out a lot of information about a company from a "people" perspective. There are also a lot of resources available online that can give you information and insight into a company.

The Lists

When I was working in staffing, I was told that I needed to come up with my lead list. I was allowed to add any company that I wanted to my lead list, as long as another staffing team member had not already identified that they were actively working with that company. As a recruiter, it was my job to find companies who were hiring, much in the same way that a job seeker does while they are in transition.

You gain so much valuable information by asking the right questions when you are out networking (but that is another workbook).So, for the purpose of this workbook, I'll focus on what I did to find the organizations using online search tools.

There are some very well known lists available that are published on an annual basis. It may take you a little bit of cross referencing, -but you can quickly identify which of these companies are in the city that you are looking to work within.

The two most well known lists are:

Inc. 500 – www.inc.com

(Per Wikipedia) – This list is an annual ranking of the country's top 5,000 fastest-growing, private companies and also features a special ranking of the top ten percent of the list—the Inc. 500. The Inc. 5000 includes the Inc. 500 but digs deeper to offer the most comprehensive look ever at the entrepreneurial engine driving the U.S. economy in the 5,000 fastest growing companies in America. The Inc. 5000 is ranked according to percentage revenue growth over a four-year period. To qualify, companies must have been founded and generating revenue by the first week of the starting calendar year, and therefore able to show four full calendar years of sales. Additionally, they had to be U.S.-based, privately held, and independent—not subsidiaries or divisions of other companies—as of December 31 of the last year measured. Revenue in the initial year must have been at least $200,000, and revenue in the most recent year must have been at least $2 million.

Fortune 500 - http://money.cnn.com/magazines/fortune/fortune500/

(Per Wikipedia) – The Fortune 500 is an annual list compiled and published by Fortune magazine that ranks the top 500 U.S. closely held and public corporations as ranked by their gross revenue after adjustments made by Fortune to exclude the impact of excise taxes companies collect. The list includes publicly and privately-held companies for which revenues are publicly available.

In addition to these lists, many different publications run other lists like "Best Places to Work," "Fastest Growing Companies," "Emerging 100," "Top 100 …" *etc.* Doing a simple Google Search for your area should help to showcase some of those lists.

Another great source of company lists is the publication group "BizJournals" (www.bizjournals.com). They currently have 68 markets where they operate. You can order a Book of Lists for your market at (http://www.bizjournals.com/bookoflists/). For job seekers, I would suggest that you go to your local library and ask for a version for you to review. Not every company in the book will be helpful to you and the cost of the books is significant. Instead, you can scan through all of the lists that are available in the library copy and you can jot down the names (or copy the pages) that interest you. The Book of Lists table of contents is available for you to review free of charge on the website.

Another great place to find some great lists is via the Chamber of Commerce for your area. Frequently the Chamber will make company lists available in order to encourage more companies to move to your city.

Financial Research

For publicly traded companies, there is a lot of financial research available. However, you can still find some information on private companies as well.

Some of the companies that I recommend are:

- Hoover's (www.hoover's.com)
- Businessweek (http://investing.businessweek.com/research/company/overview/overview.asp)
- Forbes (http://www.forbes.com/)
- Fortune (http://money.cnn.com/magazines/fortune/)
- Yahoo Finance (http://finance.yahoo.com/)

Most of these sites have a limited amount of information available to you for free. If you would like more detailed information, these sites will provide it for a fee. I find in most cases that the free search gives you plenty of information.

Competitive Research

Many of the tools that list financial information will also list company competitors. Reviewing a company's competitors is another great way to expand your list of potential companies that you might be interested in.

One tool that I particularly like when researching high level information on a company does a good job of listing competitors is Zoom Info.

Zoom Info – http://www.zoominfo.com

Once you start doing a simple search of competitors, you will uncover other tools and results that might be helpful to you.

Press Releases

An additional aid in understanding what is going on within a company is to read their press releases. You can gather a wealth of insight about a company by its press releases. Frequently, press releases contain information on new product offerings, sales wins, funding information, and key hires. For publicly traded companies, you will also see financial results.

Press releases will help you learn about new companies that you may not be aware of. They can tell you when a company secures new funding. They can tell you when a company moves locations. They can tell you when a company gets a big new client. Keep an eye on press releases going out in your area to help you to grow your list of potential companies.

Bizjournals (www.bizjournals.com) is a great place to read press releases. You can subscribe to a feed that will send you information every time a new article is published. The business section of your local paper will also include press releases. And of course, always check the News and Information in the About section of your target companies' websites.

A site called Texas Tech Pulse (www.texastechpulse.com) puts out any press releases regarding tech related companies in Texas. In Austin, a local entrepreneur produces Austin Startup (www.AustinStartup.com), which he uses to put out press releases for any of the entrepreneur-based companies in Austin. He created the list because everyone was always asking him for late breaking news about the startup community and he got tired of sending out a bunch of individual emails. So instead, he now just publishes it to one place for everyone to have access to.

I'm sure that neither Texas nor Austin is unique. Simply do a search to see if you have similar press release aggregators in your area. I subscribe to a lot of different press release feeds. I think it's a lot of fun to watch them over the course of the day. One organization will break the news and over the course of the day the others will pick it up.

Press releases are also a great reason to contact someone you know who works within an organization. Everyone loves to hear words of congratulations. Sometimes I have even told my friends about a press release within their company before they knew about it. It's a great way to stay visible to people without having to constantly ask them if a new opportunity has opened up.

Google Tools

Google is always coming up with new tools to help people to search for more information. While most people know about the general web search, the image search, and the map search, few people are paying attention to these new tools that have recently become available. Here are a few that I think can help you a lot in your job search.

Google Blog Search

http://blogsearch.google.com

Google Blog Search will allow you to search a variety of different blogs to find out who is saying something about a company in a blog. You will get information regarding a company's official blog (if they have one) along with what other people who are writing blogs are saying. This is a good way to get candid information on an organization.

Google News Search

http://news.google.com

The Google News Search allows you to search when a company has information in a news report. Frequently these are all of the variety of associated press conversations. Sometimes you will also find press releases using this tool.

Google Alerts

At the bottom of many searches there is a place to set up a Google Alert. This is an email that gets sent to you every time the search criteria show up anywhere on Google. You can also set up an alert from scratch at (http://www.google.com/alerts).

I have personally set up a Google Alert for both my name and my business. I want to know every time something new has been added to the Google search index that has my name associated with it.

This is also a great way to stay cutting edge on information about a company that you are targeting. If you can come to them and tell them about things you're read on the web that they may not have known, it shows that you have a definite interest in their company. You might not want to share everything you know at the first meeting, however.

Other Social Media

More and more companies are becoming involved in the social media. It will be interesting to see how this evolves over time. Some companies have entire departments that are responsible for paying attention to what is being said about the organization via social media. A niche in the high tech industry is devoted to building tools to help the companies "listen" and parse through the massive amounts of data created through social media channels. Unless this is an area of interest to you, I don't think you need to go into this much detail about an organization during your job search. What I do think is interesting regarding social media and companies that you are targeting is WHAT THEY ARE SAYING about themselves using social media.

Many companies have created a Twitter account to blast information out to people. You do not have to have a Twitter account (www.twitter.com) in order to read that company information. If you have many companies you're tracking, you probably should create an account and "follow" the companies. Frequently you can go to a company's website and click on the little "t" icon and go directly to their feed. Some companies even have multiple people talking about their company. This is a great way for you to get information about what the company is publicly saying about themselves. You can even "tweet" back to them to start a conversation or "retweet" what they are saying so that you show you're interested without starting a conversation.

Some companies have created a Facebook Fan Page in order to push out information about themselves. This information is frequently available to the public as well. If you already have a Facebook account (www.Facebook.com) you may want to "like" the page so you can keep up with what they are saying. Do remember that any company you "like" will know that you are interested in them.

Understand that social media is a very new idea for most companies and organizations. People are still struggling with how to use it effectively. Many companies still do not have a social media presence. It's much like in 1996 when the World Wide Web was starting to be robust and companies started to create websites. It took some time for the trend to catch on (and to know what to do with a webpage); today many companies launch their websites before they even launch their businesses.

Use social media in order to add to your knowledge of a company, rather than relying on it as the sole source of information about it.

Social Media, the Web, and YOU

While we're on the topic of researching information about companies using social media, I feel I should also take the time to point out that when a company is interested in you they will reverse the process and do whatever research they can on you. Because of this, you should do is Google yourself to find out what they will see. If you already have an active presence on the web or through social media channels, you should Google yourself frequently. Type your name in and hit enter and see what you can find out. My name is VERY unusual and there are several people out there on the web that share information with me. You can quickly spot whether it's me in Austin, Texas or if it's someone with my name in Wisconsin or Australia. Sometimes it isn't so easy to tell which available information is specifically about you.

I've heard stories of people who have a name that has become scandalous for any number of reasons. Someone who happens to share their name has been very newsworthy and notorious. In that case, there's nothing you can do about it except address it before it ever becomes an issue. Typically people won't do a detailed web search on you until you get into the later stages of the interview process. If you are one of those people who needs to explain your search results, find a time that is appropriate to bring it up so that it does not become the issue that knocks you out of the running for the job.

You should also consider what your social media presence is saying about you. I've already touched on the professionalism that you should portray using LinkedIn. You should also consider what you are saying anywhere that is accessible online. No matter how much privacy control you try to enforce for your Twitter, Facebook, Flickr, *etc.* accounts, your information is available publicly should someone choose to look hard enough for it.

When I am researching information about a candidate I always go out and look them up on Facebook. I'll look through the variety of people that might be them and I'll see what I can find out. Sometimes people make their profiles available only to friends, and sometimes they don't. If can see their friend list, and I have friends who are mutual (and with 600 friends on Facebook I frequently find one) I have one more name of someone I can contact to about my candidate. I can also look at my friend's feed to see if they have ever mentioned or tagged that individual within their own information. It's publicly available, and there's nothing illegal about it.

I have heard of a recent phenomenon where companies have been requesting a candidate's login credentials on Facebook. It is illegal to require someone to do this. However, if it is a company that you are really interested in then you might decide to comply. If they are monitoring your Facebook during the hiring process you can bet that they will continue to monitor you through the rest of your time with the company. Make sure this is the kind of culture that you want to work within.

Twitter is set up to be a public feed. Be careful how strongly you express your opinions in that forum. It may be another cause of your de-selection. I frequently talk about the football team for my alma mater. If I were interviewing for a job with someone who went to a different university, they may not be so interested in me if I was not behaving in a sportsman like fashion. So, I try to be careful when tossing insults even if they are made in jest. My enthusiasm for my college team may not rule me out, but if the hiring manager is down to the wire and trying to decide between two candidates, they will pick the less controversial candidate.

Another good tool for researching people is PIPL (www.pipl.com). I'm sure there are other tools out there like it. PIPL is a good aggregator for information about people. It will pull in social media, pictures, web postings, *etc.* It's another good place for you to go and look yourself up so that you know what might be out there.

Remember that social media and web searches are normally to help an organization to rule you out rather than rule you in. So, be cautious about what is posted out there about you and make sure you know about any dark marks so that you can provide a reasonable explanation for them.

Searching Posted Positions

Reviewing posted positions is helpful in your job search because it lets you know which positions a company is hiring for. You can find posted positions on company web sites, job boards, job aggregators, and on social media sites liked LinkedIn. Keep in mind that any posted position may not really be available, and that only six percent of those hired find their next position exclusively through posted positions.

Tips:
1. In this economy, DO NOT apply to a position electronically unless an individual with insight into the company tells you to
2. Dismiss any posting that is older than a month
3. Remember that many jobs are not posted electronically

Keep these tips in mind when working with job boards. Use them to find your information but don't let the Apply button be your only way into the organization.

Job Boards

Although there are several job boards out there, here are a few that are the most frequently used:

Career Builder (www.careerbuilder.com)
Monster (www.monster.com)
Dice (www.dice.com)

Aggregators

Aggregators are tools that pull together information from a variety of different places all at the same time. The technology sorts through job boards, recruiter sites and company job postings. Take care; frequently you will see the same job duplicated by several aggregators.

Indeed (www.indeed.com)
Simply Hired (www.simplyhired.com)
Jobing.com (www.jobing.com)

LinkedIn

You can use the "Job Search" functionality to search jobs in a variety of categories on LinkedIn.

- Location
- Experience Level
- Date Posted
- Job Title
- Company
- Job Function
- Industry

Now, Go Out and Get that Job!

Now that you've been through this workbook you should be at a point where you can:

1) Identify the company categories that you are most interested in
2) Identify the companies that you want to work for in your company categories
3) Establish an accountability group which can help keep you on track to reach your goals
4) Establish good daily habits that will allow you to meet your goals
5) Identify the problems that you solve for an organization
6) Create referrals via Internal Champions, Headhunters, and Recruiters.

You should have moved past a place where you are guessing about what you want to do and where you want to do it. You should have a clear, laser focus on the organization that you want to work for and know exactly what you are going to do to help that organization.

You are now armed with tools and information that you can use to become better equipped for the roles you want and how to get around the automated application process so that you can talk to real live human beings who want to help you with your job search process.

If you find that you are taking a survival job, do not stop this discovery process. Continue to use the techniques you've learned to get you to the job you love faster.

It may take a little while to get the ball rolling, but once it starts, if you keep up the momentum and keep using alternatives to the Apply button, you will quickly find yourself in the job that you love.

ALTERNATIVES TO THE APPLY BUTTON

APPENDIX

Daily Habit Completion Tracker

Keep track of which Daily Habits you complete every day and which ones you still need to work on. After 21 days, if the habit feels routine, you can always add in new daily habits in order to make you more successful. If you find something you never complete, you might consider taking on a different daily habit.

Daily Habit	1	2	3	4	5	6	7	8	9	10
Day 1										
Day 2										
Day 3										
Day 4										
Day 5										
Day 6										
Day 7										
Day 8										
Day 9										
Day 10										
Day 11										
Day 12										
Day 13										
Day 14										
Day 15										
Day 16										
Day 17										
Day 18										
Day 19										
Day 20										
Day 21										

Reasons for Non-Completion:

Accountability Meeting Notes

Date of Meeting
Accountability Partner
Tasks that I committed to during our last meeting (completed items designated with a checkmark)
Wins and Successes since our last meeting
Reasons why any tasks have remained uncompleted
Challenges and Obstacles since our last meeting

Possible Solutions discussed during our meeting

Tasks that I commit to complete before our next meeting

Accountability Partner Action Items (if any)

Next Meeting Time/Date

Other Notes

Accountability Notes – Template

Date of Meeting
Accountability Partner
Tasks that I committed to during our last meeting (completed items designated with a checkmark)
Wins and Successes since our last meeting
Reasons why any tasks have remained uncompleted
Challenges and Obstacles since our last meeting

Possible Solutions discussed during our meeting

Tasks that I commit to complete before our next meeting

Accountability Partner Action Items (if any)

Next Meeting Time/Date

Other Notes

Accountability Notes – Template

Date of Meeting
Accountability Partner
Tasks that I committed to during our last meeting (completed items designated with a checkmark)
Wins and Successes since our last meeting
Reasons why any tasks have remained uncompleted
Challenges and Obstacles since our last meeting

Possible Solutions discussed during our meeting
Tasks that I commit to complete before our next meeting
Accountability Partner Action Items (if any)
Next Meeting Time/Date
Other Notes

Accountability Notes - Template

Date of Meeting
Accountability Partner
Tasks that I committed to during our last meeting (completed items designated with a checkmark)
Wins and Successes since our last meeting
Reasons why any tasks have remained uncompleted
Challenges and Obstacles since our last meeting

Possible Solutions discussed during our meeting

Tasks that I commit to complete before our next meeting

Accountability Partner Action Items (if any)

Next Meeting Time/Date

Other Notes

Accountability Notes - Template

Date of Meeting
Accountability Partner
Tasks that I committed to during our last meeting (completed items designated with a checkmark)
Wins and Successes since our last meeting
Reasons why any tasks have remained uncompleted
Challenges and Obstacles since our last meeting

Possible Solutions discussed during our meeting

Tasks that I commit to complete before our next meeting

Accountability Partner Action Items (if any)

Next Meeting Time/Date

Other Notes